TABLE OF CONTENTS

INTRODUCTION 4

CHAPTER ONE 6

    Getting Started With Cryptocurrencies 6

    5 Benefits of Trading Cryptocurrencies.................. 10

    Practical Tips on How to Trade Cryptocurrencies 14

    The "Experts" Are Getting Crypto All Wrong 18

CHAPTER TWO 24

    Should You Invest in Bitcoin?................................. 24

    Thinking of Investing? Think the Bitcoin Way 27

    6 Most Common Mistakes That New Bitcoin Traders Make 32

    The Best Bitcoin Trading Platforms........................ 34

CONCLUSION 38

INTRODUCTION

Would you like to invest any kind of your hard-earned money in crypto-currencies? If so, before making the final decision, make sure you know you meet the requirements. You could risk losing your money without considering important factors. There are a lot of cryptocurrencies, like Blockchain or Bitcoin, out there. We are going to share with you a few tips in this guide that you can follow before depositing your money.

Investing in the market space for cryptocurrencies is often complex, especially for conventional investors. This is because it needs the use of emerging technology, instruments, and acceptance of certain new ideas to invest directly in Cryptocurrency. You would need to have a good understanding of what to do and what to expect if you want to dip your toes in the world of Cryptocurrencies. Buying and selling cryptocurrencies, whether it's Bitcoin, Litecoin, Ethereum, or any of the 1300 tokens, allows you to select an exchange that deals with the items you like.

Bitcoins have gained widespread popularity as a modern type of digitalized cryptocurrency. Individuals are now seeking to know how to purchase and store bitcoins with a range of online payment methods to buy something. Make sure you weigh a lot of factors if you want to invest in Bitcoin. This decision should be based on a sound technical and thorough assessment and review. You don't want your hard-earned money to be unsafe.

CHAPTER ONE

GETTING STARTED WITH CRYPTOCURRENCIES

Investing in the market space for cryptocurrencies is often complex, especially for conventional investors. This is because it needs the use of emerging technology, instruments, and acceptance of certain new ideas to invest directly in cryptocurrency.

You would need to have a good understanding of what to do and what to expect if you want to dip your toes in the world of Cryptocurrencies.

Buying and selling cryptocurrencies, whether it's Bitcoin, Litecoin, Ethereum, or any of the 1300 tokens, allows you to select an exchange that deals with the items you like.

Bitcoin leads crypto space so dominantly which the words crypto and bitcoin are often used interchangeably, becoming the most popular decentralized cryptocurrency. The truth, however, is that there are also other cryptocurrencies that can be relied on to make crypto-investments.

Litecoin

Litecoin is an open-source, the decentralized payment network that operates without an intermediary, often referred to as 'silver to Bitcoin's gold.'

How does it differ from Bitcoin to Litecoin? Well, both are equivalent in many respects, but Litecoin's block generation is much faster than Bitcoin's. This opens up the world's investors to consider Litecoin.

In 2011, Charlie Lee, a former Google engineer, created Litecoin. While Litecoin does not have Bitcoin's anonymity technology, recent studies have shown that Litecoin is favored because of its durability after bitcoin. The Bitcoin SegWit technology is another aspect that favors Litecoin, implying secure peer-to-peer trading of currencies without requiring exchange participation.

Ethereum

Ethereum, which was introduced in 2015, is a decentralized software framework that allows distributed applications and smart contracts to work without intervention from third parties. The currency is the ether, as an accelerator inside the platform of the ethereum. In the room of leading cryptocurrencies, Ethereum. After Bitcoin, it is the second-most preferred option.

Zcash

In the latter part of 2016, Zcash gained popularity and concentrated on solving the issue of anonymous transactions. Let's take it as, "if Bitcoin is like HTTP for money, Zcash is HTTPS" to understand the currency.

In order to preserve the integrity, anonymity, and protection of transactions, the currency provides an option of shielded transactions. This implies that, in the form of encrypted code, investors can pass data.

Dash

Dash, known originally as darkcoin, is a more selective clone of bitcoin. It was released by Evan Duffield under the name Xcoin in January 2014. It is also known as the Independent Decentralized Organization, or simply the DAO. The coin was intended to remove many of Bitcoin's prevalent limitations. At present, Bitcoin has won a major role in the cryptocurrency room.

Cryptocurrency is the alternative to virtual currency that promises secured and anonymous transactions through peer-to-peer networking. Making the correct investment at the right moment is the secret to making a lot of money. In contrast to making regular cash, cryptocurrency models act as a decentralized digital mechanism without involving any middle man. The continuous operation is published, controlled, and endorsed by the community peer network in this distributed cryptocurrency process. The cryptocurrency is known for its fast transactions, such as digital wallets and other media, over any other mode.

Other top cryptocurrencies, in addition to the above, include Monero (XMR), Bitcoin Cash (BCH). Ripple and EOS (XRP).

While bitcoin is the setter of trends and leads the race, other currencies have also formed their important role and are rising daily in choice. The other cryptos would have a long way to stay, given the trend, and may soon give Bitcoin the real tough time to retain its role.

5 BENEFITS OF TRADING CRYPTOCURRENCIES

You have to guess whether a market you have selected would go up or down in value when it comes to cryptocurrency trading. And the odd thing is that the digital property was never owned by you. The trading is actually conducted with derivative products such as CFDs. Let's look at the advantages of dealing with cryptocurrencies. To find out more, read on.

Volatility

While cryptocurrency is a new business, the short-lived speculative interest makes it very unpredictable. The price of bitcoin fell from $19,378 in 2018, in just one year, to $5851. The value of other digital currencies, however, is pretty steady, which is good news.

The uncertainty of that value of the crypto-currency was what makes this environment so exciting. A lot of opportunity for trader was created by price fluctuations. This comes, however, with many dangers as well. Therefore, just make sure you do the homework and put together the risk management plan if you intending to explore the market.

Business Hours

The market is always open 24/7 for trade, and it is not controlled by any government. In addition, transactions are carried out between buyers and sellers worldwide. When the infrastructural changes take place, there might be brief downtimes.

Improved Liquidity

Liquidity refers to how easy it is possible to sell a digital currency for cash. This function is important because it allows for faster transaction times, better precision, and better pricing. In general, when financial transactions happen through numerous exchanges, the market is kind of illiquid. Therefore, small companies would bring about major price changes.

Leveraged Exposure

"You could open a position on since CFD trading being considered a leveraged asset, what we call "margin". In this case, a percentage of the economic value is the value of the deposit. So, without spending a lot of money, you can enjoy great exposure to the market.

At the moment of its closing, the loss or benefit will represent the value of the place. Therefore, by spending a small amount of money, you can gain massive profits if you trade on margin. It also amplifies losses, however, which can surpass your deposit on a trade. Therefore, you should make sure you are taking into account your investment in CFDs before investing in account the overall value of the position.

It is also important to ensure which you follow a solid plan for risk management, which must include proper limits and stops.

Quick Account Opening

Make sure that you're doing it through an exchange if you want to purchase cryptocurrencies. All you have to do is sign up and hold the currency in your wallet for an exchange account. Remember that this method will take a great deal of time and effort and be restrictive. However, the rest of the process will be very smooth and free of complications once the account is established.

Long story short, these are some of the most popular advantages of investing in cryptocurrencies here and now.

Practical Tips on How to Trade Cryptocurrencies

For some time now, to get a sense of where a market is heading, I have been closely watching the success of cryptocurrencies. My elementary school teacher's routine taught me that where you wake up, then pray, brush the teeth, and have your breakfast has changed a little to waking up, praying, and the hitting web (start with the coinmarketcap) to see what crypto assets are in the red.

The beginning of 2018 for altcoins and relatable properties was not a lovely one. Their success was crippled by bankers' frequent opinions that the crypto bubble was about to blow. Nevertheless, ardent cryptocurrency followers were still "HODLing" on, and they are reaping high, to be told the reality.

Bitcoin recently retraced to nearly $5000; Bitcoin Money came close to the $500, while at $300, Ethereum found harmony. Apart from the newcomers who were still in a stage of excitement, nearly every coin was struck. Bitcoin is back on track and trading at $8900 as of this writing. Since the upward trend began, many other cryptos have doubled, and the market cap is resting at $400 billion from the recent $250 billion crests.

The tips below will help you out whether you're slowly warming up with cryptocurrencies as well as wish to become a good trader.

Convenient guidance on how to exchange cryptocurrencies

- **Start modestly**

You have learned the cryptocurrency prices were skyrocketing already. You have probably also received the news that this upward trend will not last a long time. Some naysayers generally go ahead, mainly respected bankers and economists, to tag them get-rich-quick schemes with no solid base.

Such news would cause you to invest in such a hurry and not apply restraint. A little study of market dynamics and investment in trigger-worthy currencies will guarantee you good returns. Do not spend all your hard-earned money on these assets, no matter what you do.

Understand how exchanges work

A man went on to trade in an exchange that had zero thoughts about how it operates. This is a perilous pass. Before signing up, or even at least before you begin trading, always check the platform you plan to use. Take the opportunity to learn how the dashboard looks if they have a dummy account to the play around with.

Do not rely on all-trading.

There are many over 1400 cryptocurrencies to be sold, but all of them are difficult to deal with. Spreading the portfolio to the large number of cryptos would reduce the income that you can handle effectively. Only pick a couple of them, learn about them more, and how to get their trade signals.

• Stay sober

There are volatile cryptocurrencies. This is their bane as well as their boon. You have to realize as a trader that wild price swings are inevitable. Uncertainty on whether one is an inefficient trader when making a pass. To be sure when to conduct a trade, exploit hard data and other analysis methods.

Effective traders belong to numerous online forums where market dynamics and signals are debated in cryptocurrency discussions. Yes, your information will be adequate, but for more specific data, you need to rely on other traders.

- **Diversify meaningfully**

Virtually everybody will tell you to grow your portfolio, but nobody would remind you to the deal with real-world uses of currencies. There are a few lousy coins you can play with for fast bucks, but those who fix existing issues are the best cryptos to deal with. Coins with uses from the real world tend to be less volatile.

Do not diversify too late or too early. And make sure you know the market cap, price shifts, and regular trading volumes before you make a move to buy any crypto-asset. The way to harvest large amounts of these digital assets is to maintain a balanced portfolio.

The "Experts" Are Getting Crypto All Wrong

It doesn't matter unless you just lost your shirt on bitcoin. And it is possible that the "experts" you see in the press don't tell you why.

Currently, bitcoin's collapse is great... And it means that we can all stop worrying completely about cryptocurrencies.

Bitcoin's death...

In a year or so, people won't care about bitcoin as they are now in the supermarket or bus road. This is why. Here is why.

The result of justified anger is Bitcoin. His creator specifically said that the cryptocurrency responded to state abuses of fiat currencies such as the dollar and euro. The plan was to have an independent, peer-to-peer payment system based on a virtual currency not degradable since a limited number of them existed.

The dream has been thrown away for raw speculation for many years. Ironically, most people really care about bitcoin, as the way to get more fiat currency looks fast! You don't even own it because you would like to buy pizzas or gas.

In addition to being a lousy way to electronically transact - it is agonizingly slow -, the popularity of bitcoin as a speculative play has made it unnecessary as a currency. Why would someone invest it if it was so easy to appreciate? Who will consider one as it easily depreciates?

Bitcoin is also a major emission source. The processing of a single transaction takes only 351-kilowatt hours of energy, which also releases 172 kg of carbon dioxide into the atmosphere. It's enough to fuel one household in the United States for a year. The energy all bitcoin mining has consumed to date will produce almost four million U.S. households a year.

Paradoxically, Bitcoin's popularity – not its liberal intentions – as an old-fashioned speculative game has drawn government repression.

South Korea, China, Switzerland, Germany, and France have or are considering prohibitions or limits on bitcoin trading. Several intergovernmental organizations, in the apparent bubble, have called for collective action. The Exchange Commission and U.S. Securities, once likely to allow financial derivatives based on bitcoin, now seems reluctant.

'The European Union imposes tighter legislation to deter money laundering and terrorist funding on virtual currency platforms.

One day we will see an approved, practical cryptocurrency, but it won't be bitcoin.

There was a mistake. However, a rise in crypto assets.

Nice. Good. Moving beyond bitcoin helps us to see where the true worth of crypto assets resides. This is how. Here's how.

You need tokens to use the New York subway system. You can't buy anything else with them... You could sell them to anyone who wanted more than you to use the subway.

In reality, if subway tokens were restricted, a vibrant market might arise for them. They could also trade much more than they originally cost. It all depends on how much people want to use the metro.

That, in short, is the most exciting scenario for "cryptocurrencies" other than bitcoin. They're not money; they're tokens, if you like, "crypto-tokens," They're not used as a popular currency. They are only good on the platform they have been built for.

If these platforms offer useful services, people would want those crypto-tokens to decide their costs. In other words, crypto-to-tokens would have value insofar as people value items from their related forum for them.

This makes them actual assets with inherent value – so they can be used to get something people value. That means you can accurately anticipate such crypto-tokens from a stream of revenues or services. Critically speaking, you will calculate this potential yield against the crypto-token price as you do when measuring an inventory's price/earnings ratio.

By comparison, Bitcoin has no intrinsic value. It has just a price - the price of supply and demand. It cannot create potential revenue sources, and for it, you cannot calculate anything like a P/E ratio.

It'll be useless one day because it doesn't really get you anything.

Other Crypto Assets Are the Future

The crypto-token ether definitely appears like a currency. It is traded under the ETH code on cryptocurrency exchanges. The Greek uppercase Xi character is its symbol. It is mined in a similar method to bitcoin (but less energy-intensive).

Ether's not a currency, though. Its creators describe it as "a fuel for operating a distributed the application platform Ethereum. It is the form of payment made by this client of the platform to the machines executing the requested operations."

Ether tokens allow you to access one of the most advanced distributed computer networks in the world. It's so promising that big corporations fall all over to build realistic, real-world uses.

Since most traders don't really understand or care about their true intent, the price of ether has bubbled and splashed like bitcoin in the last few weeks.

However, ether would ultimately return to a stable price, depending on the demand for computer services it can "buy" for people. This price is a true value that can be valued in the future. There will be a potential market for it and ETFs, so everyone will be able to determine the value behind it over time, just as we do for inventories.

CHAPTER TWO

SHOULD YOU INVEST IN BITCOIN?

This section is for you if you are curious what Bitcoin is and if you should invest in it. The value of one Bitcoin was just 5 cents in 2010. Quick forward, and its value reached $20,000 in 2017. Again, over the next 24 hours, the price fell to $8,000, causing a massive loss for the currency holders.

This will help you to read if you have been trying to find out more about Bitcoin. Around 24% of Americans know what it is, according to estimates. The currency still has a value of over $152 billion, however. That is one of the most common reasons for this item's popularity. Let's know what it is and whether it's something you can believe in.

What is Bitcoin?

In simple terms, one of the digital currencies is Bitcoin. A cryptocurrency is known as a digital currency. In 2008, the word was coined by an unknown person during the financial crisis.

A digital currency account that can be accessed online is close to your checking account. It's a digital currency, in other words, that can be accessed but cannot be reached. You have no physical representation, either, in the case of Bitcoin. All of the money is only available in digital form. There is nobody there to control this kind of currency. In the same way, no organization controls the network, and the tokens are exchanged through a complex software system between individuals. The whole thing, instead, is decentralized and is run by a computer network.

It's important to remember that for anything you want to purchase, you cannot use these tokens to pay. In reality, you can only use it to buy online from certain sellers or shops. But it can be sold in conventional currencies or in cash. More and more businesses, however, are starting to embrace Bitcoin and other cryptocurrencies. Expedia and

Overstock, for example, embrace this from users. One of the key characteristics of this type of money is that it is absolutely private and untraceable to the transaction. That's one of the many reasons this digital type of money is preferred by most people.

Should you put money on Bitcoin?

Remember: make sure you understand the risks associated with this method before you want to invest in Bitcoin or any other digital currency. One of the big risks is uncertainty. It means that in 24 hours, the value of your money will dramatically fluctuate. The rise or fall in value can potentially be as much as 30 percent. Another issue is that, according to most analysts, most of the digital currencies that can be used today will lose their value within five years.

We recommend that you invest only so that you can afford to lose, to be on the safe side. If you have $1,000, for instance, you can spend $10. And it won't cause any financial difficulties for you if you lose that number.

Hopefully, now, you understand what Bitcoin is and whether your hard-earned cash should be invested in it.

Remember: a lot of money should not be spent, or you will get into the serious financial trouble down the road.

THINKING OF INVESTING? THINK THE BITCOIN WAY

Bitcoin has become one of the main regular news headlines - as a fast get rich scheme, the end of banking, the birth of a genuinely foreign currency, as the end of the planet, or as a world-enhancing technology. What is Bitcoin, though?

In short, you can assume that Bitcoin is the first decentralized money system used for online transactions, but digging a little deeper would probably be useful.

In general, we all know what 'money' is and what it is used for. The most critical problem that existed before Bitcoin in the use of money relates to its centralization and regulation by a single person, the centralized banking system. An anonymous developer, who goes by the alias 'Satoshi Nakamoto' to bring decentralization to money on a global scale, invented Bitcoin in 2008/2009. The idea is that with no difficulty or fees, the currency could be exchanged through foreign borders, the checks and balances would be spread across the globe (rather than only on the heads of private companies or governments), and money would become more egalitarian and available to all equally.

How did they start Bitcoin?

Satoshi, an anonymous researcher, began the idea of bitcoin, and cryptocurrency in general, in 2009. The reason for its invention was to address the problem of centralization in the use of money that depended on banks and computers, a question that was not satisfied with by many computer scientists. Achieving decentralization has been attempted without success since the late 90s, so it was overwhelmingly accepted when Satoshi published a paper offering a solution in 2008. Bitcoin has become the common currency for internet users today and has created thousands of 'altcoins' (non-Bitcoin cryptocurrencies).

How Bitcoin is made?

Via a process called mining, Bitcoin is made. Bitcoin is produced through 'mining' much as paper money is made by printing, and gold is extracted from the earth. Mining includes solving and applying complex mathematical issues to a public ledger regarding blocks using computers. When it started, all one needed to mine was a basic CPU (like your home computer), but the level of complexity has increased dramatically, and now you will need advanced hardware to extract Bitcoin, including high-end graphics processing units (GPUs).

How am I going to invest?

First, you have to open a trading platform account and build a wallet; some examples can be found by searching Google for 'Bitcoin trading platform' - they typically have names that include 'coin' or 'business.' You click on the assets after entering one of these sites, and then click on crypto to select your preferred currency. On any site, there are a lot of indicators that are very important, and before investing, you should be sure to observe them.

Simply purchase and hold

While mining is the easiest and simplest way in earning Bitcoin, there are many hustle involved, and it is inaccessible to most of us because of the cost of electricity and specialized computer hardware. To stop all this, make it easy for yourself to enter the sum you want from the bank directly and click "buy," then sit back and watch as the investment increases in according to the shift in price. This is called an exchange and takes place on many exchange platforms available today, with the ability to swap between various different fiat currencies (GBP, AUD, USD, etc.) and various crypto coins (Litecoin, Ethereum, Bitcoin, etc.).

Trading Bitcoin

If you really are familiar with bonds, stocks, or Forex exchanges, then you can easily understand crypto-trading. There are Bitcoin brokers that you can choose from. The platforms to provide you with currency pairs of Bitcoin-fiat or fiat-Bitcoin, such as trading Bitcoins for the U.S. dollars.

Bitcoin as Shares

Organizations are also set up to encourage you to purchase shares in companies invested in Bitcoin - these businesses swap back and forth, and you only invest in them and wait for your monthly benefits. These businesses actually pool and invest on their behalf with digital money from various investors.

Why do you have to invest in Bitcoin?

As you can see, as mentioned above, investing in Bitcoin needs you to have some basic knowledge of the currency. It entails risk, as with all investments! The question about whether or not to invest depends entirely mostly on the individual. However, if I were to provide advice, I could advise in favor of investing in Bitcoin because Bitcoin continues to develop, although there has been one sense.

6 Most Common Mistakes That New Bitcoin Traders Make

Are you thinking of beginning in the crypto-trading world? If so, ensure that the most common errors are avoided. By making these errors, you would be better than most crypto traders. Interestingly, almost every trader does not even know these errors. Let's find out some famous mistakes without further ado. Read on to learn more.

1. Making emotional decisions

Beginners prefer emotionally to exchange. However, the thing is that your feelings have nothing to do with trading. Currently, if you determine on the basis of your feelings, you are on the path to failure.

2. Buying high and selling low

Another common error that beginners make is to buy high and sell low. During this business, you don't want to get gullible. You must have to buy low and sell high. This is the only way to make a Bitcoin profit trading.

3. Selling at once

Due to the above two errors, beginners purchase or sell their Bitcoins at once instead of purchasing them and selling them gradually in small amounts. If you are asking an experienced investor, they will ask you to sell 20% of your Bitcoin profit after 50%. The problem, however, is that new traders are too eager to sell. They don't have the money to buy dips. Some of them sell all their Bitcoins simultaneously.

4. Purchase of wrong currencies

New business is buying cryptocurrencies that use big words to make loads of promises. But they don't know that these currencies do not, in order to name a few, have technological advancements like Litecoin, NEO, Tron, and EOS. The problem is that the blockchains are very centralized. Maybe you want to stop them.

5. Through so many buckets, put your eggs

Due to the previous error, beginners prefer to invest in several cryptocurrencies. This isn't a smart idea because it will make profits hard for you. You should preferably invest in 3 to 4 coins. You can't afford to place all your eggs in loads of sackcloth in the cryptocurrency world.

6. In one basket, put all eggs

Another common error is to put your eggs in one basket. You should preferably have a well-diversified portfolio. In addition, you do not want to deposit or swap all of the cryptocurrencies of yours in the same wallet. What you have to do is use at least three wallets. This helps you safeguard your investment.

THE BEST BITCOIN TRADING PLATFORMS

Cryptocurrency has created not only the quickest way of exchanging money but also a new entity for trading and earning money separately from stocks and other commodities. Although you can buy and sell Bitcoin directly, you can also continue with Bitcoin trading platforms in cryptocurrencies. There are many exchanges where Bitcoin trade is safe and secure, and even many expanded services are offered to customers. You can select any of the exchanges for your comfort as a cryptocurrency investor or trader. However, it is recommended to look at some feedback before selecting one. Below is a short overview of the world's biggest Bitcoin exchanges.

CoinBase: It's probably one of the best established and largest Bitcoin trading exchanges for direct and wallet dual facilities. CoinBase was created in 2012 through the Y-Combinator venture finding and has expanded rapidly since then. It provides many lucrative services such as multiple deposit and withdrawal options, instant money transfers between two CoinBases, multi-signature wallet facilities for safer transfers, Bitcoin deposits for all lost, etc. CoinBase has a wide range of payment partners from Europe and the USA, which allow seamless transactions to take place. It had relatively low transaction costs and provides Bitcoin exchange along with a wide variety of Altcoin trading.

CEX.IO: Among oldest and most famous exchanges begun in 2013, as an exchange for Bitcoin trading and cloud mining facilitator in London. Its mining power subsequently expanded so tremendously that it had almost half of its mining power; however, it has now been closed. "CEX.IO" enables consumers to extend to many more Bitcoin companies and can immediately make Bitcoin available at the requested price. However, the exchange charges are a bit high, but the protection and facilities for allowing multi-currency transactions (euro, dollar, and Ruble) to buy Bitcoin are compensated.

Bitfinex: It is among the most advanced trading exchanges for seasoned cryptocurrency traders. It is especially suitable. With high Ethereum and Bitcoin liquidity, this exchange has better choices, such as leveraging, margin funding, and multiple order trading. In addition to this, Bitfinex offers customizable GUI features, various orders, including cap, pause, trailing stop, market, etc. The exchange also offers around 50 currency pairs that could be exchanged and withdrawn conveniently for anyone. One of the largest exchanges for the amount exchanged by Bitfinex provides pseudonymity for trade and needs authentication only for certain services. The only downside with this trade is that it does not support the purchase of Bitcoin or any other altcoin in fiat transactions.

Bitstamp: It was established in 2011 and is the oldest of the cryptocurrency and bitcoin trading exchanges. The most valued, because it was never under security threat even though it was older, and until recently. Bitstamp currently supports four Ethereum, Bitcoin, Litecoin, and Ripple currencies and is also available for the smartphone app, apart from the website. It provides great support for European users or traders with their Euro Banks accounts. The protection is advanced and cold, which ensures that coins are kept offline. You may also assume that any hacker cannot infiltrate. In the end, its complex user interface shows that it is not for the casual user but for professionals and provides comparatively low transaction costs.

CONCLUSION

If you want to make extra money with monetary trade, it is high time to take it seriously and learn as much as possible about foreign exchange trading currencies. There is no good alternative to studying and planning.

Currency trading is not just a purchase and sale in the market of currency pairs. If this is so easy, if you buy a low currency, if your currency is high, anyone who joins the company will benefit from it. But you can hear people losing their trade capital. How is this because systems and applications are readily available?

Learning currency trading is definitely an important component in the success of the exchange. You must be able to increase your awareness and build your skills to create strategies for your benefit. You can also use the readily available currency trading tools and optimize your income with the right education.

You will need to learn how to take calculated risks in monetary trading. Since trade is complex and sensitive, with many factors influencing currency value – the product in trade – one must be able to take advantage of the risk.

Most of all, by researching and analyzing the trading currency market, one must be able to make rapid yet sound decisions that carry money and make decent profits.

www.ingramcontent.com/pod-product-compliance
Lightning Source LLC
Chambersburg PA
CBHW030519220526
45464CB00006B/2861